Colossians

At His Feet Studies

By Hope A. Blanton and Christine B. Gordon

19Baskets

Colossians
At His Feet Studies
© 2023 by Hope A. Blanton and Christine B. Gordon
Print ISBN 978-1-946862-23-5
ePub ISBN 978-1-946862-24-2

19Baskets, Inc.
PO Box 31291
Omaha, NE 68131
https://19baskets.com

First Edition

Cover design by Will Kelly

Photography by Jen Hinrichs

Contents

At His Feet Story   1

How to Use This Study   3

1. Introduction   7

2. We Heard of Your Faith: Colossians 1:1–8   15

3. Strengthened with All Power: Colossians 1:9–14   23

4. In Him All Things Hold Together: Colossians 1:15–23   33

5. God's Mystery: Colossians 1:24–2:5   41

6. Together with Him: Colossians 2:6–15   51

7. Union with Christ: Colossians 2:16–3:4   61

8. Putting on the New Self: Colossians 3:5–17   69

9. A New Humanity: Colossians 3:18–4:6   79

10. Paul's Friends and Fellow Workers: Colossians 4:7–18   89

Works Cited   99

Acknowledgments   101

Other At His Feet Studies   103

At His Feet Story

In the summer of 2013, Hope started looking for materials for the women's fall Bible study at our church. While she found a great number of quality Bible studies, she had a hard time finding studies written for women by women who were reformed. She also had a tough time finding in-depth studies of the Scripture that didn't take a whole lot of time. In a moment of desperation, Hope asked Chris if she would be willing to co-write a study on Romans, convincing her by asking, "I mean, really, how hard could it be?" And so it began. Weekly emails back and forth, Chris deep in commentaries, Hope mulling over questions, tweaking, editing, asking, pondering. A group of women at Redeemer Presbyterian Church in Lincoln, Nebraska, patiently bore with us as we experimented with them every week and learned to find our rhythm as writers.

Two years later, Hope approached Chris again, softening her up by telling her she could choose any book she wanted: 1 Samuel it was. Old Testament narrative is the best. Another study was born. About this time, women started asking us for copies of the two studies we had written. While we were trying to send endless pdfs to people around the country via email, a pastor friend who happens to be a publisher approached us at a party, offering to publish the Bible studies. Suddenly, we had a way to get these into the hands of women who could use them. This had been the point of the whole enterprise—to help make the Bible more accessible to women. But what would the name be?

During the first century, when Jesus walked the earth, a Jewish rabbi would have been surrounded by his students, with some of the men sitting as his feet to learn and listen. This was the custom, the understood norm of the day. But in Luke 10:39, *Mary* sat at the feet of Jesus. Mary, a woman, was taught by this unconventional rabbi. Mary was given the dignity of taking in his words, his pauses, his tone. To Jesus, she was every bit as worthy of his teaching as the men in the room were—and so are we, his women students today. And so we are At His Feet Bible Studies, hoping to sit at the feet of Jesus while we study his Word.

Please find our other available studies at our website:
www.athisfeetstudies.com

How to Use This Study

There is no right way to lead a Bible study. Every Bible study group is made up of different types of people with various needs and dynamics. Below are some suggestions that might be helpful when using At His Feet Studies. Read it through. Use what you want. Forget the rest. We're glad you're here.

A different approach to a familiar method

As with many Bible studies you're familiar with, we follow a pattern of observation, interpretation, and application, but the presentation may be a little different than what you're used to. Instead of bouncing between those three tasks, we group them.

First, you will read a biblical passage, and using the Observation Questions, you'll note the people mentioned, terms used, commands given, actions taken, and so on. This is arguably the most important step, as the Word of God itself is powerful and active.

In the next section, you will interpret the biblical passage with help from seminary-trained Chris. The Interpretation section is written in the style of most commentaries, offering a verse-by-verse explanation of the biblical passage. This section is rooted in study of the original language and multiple sources, including commentaries, original language helps, sermons, theological treatises, and personal conversations with seminary professors.

Finally, you will apply the biblical text to your life, assisted by licensed therapist Hope and her heart-engaging Reflection Questions.

In this way, you will read, interpret, and then reflect on a larger passage as a whole, helping to keep the words and message in their context.

On what day do I do what?

You can read through and complete the entire study in one sitting or break it up. If you'd like to spread out your preparation a bit more, break it into three days: On day 1, read the biblical passage and complete the Observation Questions. On day 2, read the Interpretation section. On day 3, complete the Reflection Questions. You could even add a day 4 by attempting to memorize or simply meditate on the focus verse and/or write down your thoughts in the space for "Reflections, curiosities, frustrations."

How do I lead a group through this study?

It is always a good idea to read through the biblical passage out loud at the beginning of your time together. After reading the Scripture aloud, choose one or two Observation Questions and answer them as a group.

If most of your group has had a chance to read the Interpretation section on their own, ask them what stood out to them in that section and talk through parts of the commentary they may have highlighted. If you are leading a group with participants who have not had the time to read through the Interpretation section on their own, take the time to read it out loud as a group before asking this question.

Next, choose three or four of your favorite Reflection Questions and allow time for everyone who would like to offer their answers. These questions are written with the aim of both engaging your own heart and also engaging one another's hearts as you study together.

If you have the time, do all of the above and walk through all of the Reflection Questions. If you'd like, you could ask the group what questions or frustrations arose during their study.

Want an extra challenge?

Issue the challenge to your group to memorize the focus verse and say it together when you reconvene.

Questions? Reach out!

We would love to hear from you. Write us at:

athisfeetstudies@gmail.com

Study 1

Read the book of Colossians

Several years ago after much planning and research, my husband and I secretly bought our three children a puppy for Christmas. There were squeals of delight and tears of joy when a small, timid ball of fluff with big eyes and dark fur was revealed. We were all instantly in love with the puppy. Children fought over who would take him outside each hour. They bargained with each other for the privilege of feeding him. For several days he was never left alone.

After two weeks, the puppy, though still cute and cuddly, was no longer new or exciting. My kids no longer vied for his attention or fought to feed him. When asked, they took him outside more out of duty than affection. They had moved on to finding the next novel thing. This is the way of humans, is it not? We are easily bored. We love a new product or a thrilling adventure; we are afraid we'll miss out on a new encounter or interesting idea. The same was true of humans hundreds of years ago. The Colossian Christians were lured by false teachers promising a fuller spiritual experience. Though the greatness of Jesus had not changed, they were being told that there was more available, that there were practices and disciplines beyond Christ that would *really* fill them up. This letter written to the Colossians serves as a reminder that they already had the fullness of God in Christ and that he was sufficient to fill them and their lives.

Who were the Colossians?

The Colossians were first-century inhabitants of a town called Colossae in the region of Phrygia, a Roman province that corresponds to modern-day southwestern Turkey. While once a growing and important city, by the first century it had dwindled in size. The majority of people in this area were Gentiles (non-Jews) from a variety of backgrounds. Colossae was located on an important trading highway, lending itself to a diversity of religions, philosophies, and races.

It is believed that three major schools of thought—ingredients, if you will—created a religious stew that the Colossians were simmering in. Together, these three ways of thinking shaped how they practiced religion: (1) The Phrygians were a people group who dealt with their great superstition and fear of the unknown by creating mystery religions, banding together in secret groups and holding precious private information that could not be divulged to outsiders. (2) Others practiced a Hellenistic system of philosophy that held one's thoughts and beliefs in high regard, while mostly overlooking one's actual behaviors. In this philosophy, the spirit was good and to be cultivated, while the material body was evil. (3) Finally, there were the Jews, who followed the historical Jewish faith of the Old Testament. Of these three influential ways of thinking—mystery religions, Hellenism, and the Jewish faith—the Gentiles, who were the majority of the Colossian church, would have been most familiar with the first two.

Who is writing this letter and why?

Read Acts 19:1-10. Paul, the unlikely disciple and church planter, took multiple missionary journeys in order to spread the gospel among both Jews and Gentiles. During his third missionary journey, Paul spent at least two years in Ephesus, where many living in the area had the opportunity to hear the gospel (Acts 19:10). People from all over the region heard Paul preaching in Ephesus. It is probable that Epaphras, a Colossian, heard the gospel from Paul in Ephesus and took it back to his hometown. Also, in Acts 2:10 during the occasion of Pentecost, we read that there were Jews from Phrygia who were filled with the Holy Spirit and heard the apostles speaking in their own language. It is possible that some believed in Jesus or at least heard of his greatness and brought that knowledge back to Colossae.

Regardless of who the first believer was in Colossae, the little church there began to grow. The gospel that Epaphras had learned from Paul was taught, and more came to faith. Some Jews came to understand that Jesus, killed about thirty years before, was truly God and worshiped him. More Gentiles came and also believed, joining and outnumbering their Jewish brothers and sisters. It is estimated that Epaphras heard the gospel from Paul in Ephesus around 53–55 AD. By 60 AD, between five and seven years later, a new group of people had begun to infiltrate the church. These men were teaching something different, something new, something dangerous. Epaphras, worried for the spiritual health of his church, traveled to Paul personally to tell him about this new teaching and ask for pastoral help. Paul wrote this letter to the Colossians after hearing Epaphras's concerns, probably around 60–62 AD, while in prison either in Rome or Ephesus.

What was the false teaching?

Paul begins his letter with the solution to the false teaching that had begun to enter the church. What exactly the false teaching was is a question scholars argue about. Though we cannot be completely sure about the details, we can infer a few things from the language Paul uses. First, and most important, this teaching was "not according to Christ" (Colossians 2:8). As opposed to the true gospel, which is completely centered on Christ, this new teaching was not in agreement with Jesus's teaching. Second, scholars agree that the teaching was probably some mix of the three influences mentioned earlier: some sort of mystery religion elements plus Hellenistic philosophy plus Jewish tradition. It was being said that Christ was not enough, that the gospel was not sufficient to fulfill people spiritually. Paul spends his entire letter to the Colossians writing about the supremacy of Christ to combat the false teaching that was threatening the church.

How is this different from other letters Paul wrote?

Paul wrote nine letters to different churches that are included in the Bible; each letter was in response to the struggles of a particular church. For example, when the Galatians struggled with adding Jewish traditions to the requirements for salvation, Paul addressed this by teaching the doctrine of justification by faith. The Colossians were struggling to believe that Christ was sufficient for their satisfaction and spiritual life. As a solution, Paul wrote to them about the supremacy of Christ in all things.

What does this have to do with me today?

We, like the Colossians, are convinced at times that Jesus is not sufficient for our spiritual lives. Of course, we would never articulate it that way, but we can easily be tempted by products, people, or practices—or even spiritual gifts—that tell us they're necessary for a true or real understanding of the Christian life. These usually have at the core some set of practices or rules that one must follow in order to be a genuine or legitimate believer or to be able to obtain a certain level of spiritual experience. You might hear that you *must* fast from media or speak in tongues or have a radical conversion story in order to have a full Christian life.

This is not the true gospel. Jesus does not need a turbo boost. If the pursuit of a spiritual experience instead of the pursuit of Jesus becomes the center of our spiritual life, we've gotten lost.

We also get bored. Again, we wouldn't want to say it publicly, but we may come to a place where we think, "Yes, yes. I know about Jesus and salvation. Tell me something new." When we reach this place, it is never because we have exhausted his beauty, wisdom, or magnificence. It is always that we have failed to comprehend his greatness. It is never that Jesus has become less. We cannot use up or come to the end of his loveliness and majesty.

The solution to all of the above is not a new experience but rather a new vision of Christ's supremacy, kingship, and power. We need new eyes for us to see our master for who he truly is and to understand our privilege in him. What the Colossians needed and what we need is to continue in Christ, to walk in him. Colossians contains some of the richest Christological passages (sections of the Bible about the person and work of Jesus) in all of Scripture. If you are a follower of Christ, there is rich food here. This letter also spends some valuable time explaining union with Christ, meaning how we are connected to Christ and what that means for us. This is a bedrock of Christian theology.

Do you think you've exhausted the riches of Christ? Think again. Are you looking for something new to fill you spiritually? Instead, take a long look at Jesus. And then, once you are renewed by a vision of his majesty, order your life around him. Everything else will pale in comparison to who he is. Only then will your heart long to obey and begin to order your church relationships, family relationships, and all other interactions according to Christ. Only then will you find him sufficient, satisfactory, and enough to be the center of your life. When we hold the shiny new thing or practice up beside the magnificence of Christ and all of the treasure stored in him, we will see again and again that the beauty and sufficiency of Christ never fades.

Reflection Questions

1. Who is Epaphras, and what did he ask for from Paul?

2. What were the three ways of thinking that were affecting the Colossae church?

3. In your own words, how would you define the supremacy of Christ?

4. The Colossians were at risk of losing interest in the beauty and supremacy of Christ. How has that been true of you? How do you hope studying Colossians shifts that for you?

5. What are your hopes for your time studying this book of the Bible?

Reflections, curiosities, frustrations:

Study 2

We Heard of Your Faith

Read Colossians 1:1–8

Observation Questions

1. In verses 3–5a, what specifically is Paul thankful for in the lives of believers in Colossae?

2. In verses 5b–6, how does Paul describe what the gospel is doing?

3. Who is Epaphras and what has he done (verses 7–8)?

Interpretation

What would the prison-bound apostle Paul write to the church in Colossae, a group of people he had never met, in response to their founding pastor's concern for their spiritual situation? He would begin, as he often does, by orienting himself and these dear brothers and sisters to Christ. Paul begins with his own calling to follow Jesus and then reminds these believers of their own.

Verses 1–2. If you've read Paul's letters before, you may have noticed that they all have a similar structure. Just as our letters begin and end in a certain way, so ancient letter writing had a common form. The author's name came at the beginning and always had some sort of greeting that followed. Paul employs the template of his day for his own purposes. He names himself and his calling as an apostle—belonging to Christ because of God's will—and mentions his fellow worker Timothy.

The "saints" Paul addresses are not some elite group of high-achieving believers, separated from the common Christians in the city of Colossae. These men and women had the same designation that all believers in Christ hold, even today. This word does not describe their behavior or their track record of holiness. Instead, it declares their standing before God because of Christ's work on the cross. Just as Old Testament saints were referred to as God's holy people, set apart for him, so these New Testament saints enjoy the same status. If you are in Christ, his behavior and faithfulness, not your own, has earned you the title "saint" as well. The word "faithful" works the same way here. It does not describe their level of faithfulness but is a statement about who they are because of Jesus. Because they are in the family of God, they are spiritual brothers and sisters, with bonds whose strength may exceed that of a natural family.

Paul uses two locators in this verse: "in Christ" and "at Colossae." These believers are located spiritually in Christ and geographically at Colossae. While letters traditionally offered a wish for good health at this point, Paul instead inserts his desire for grace and peace from God, the only one who can ultimately supply such things.

Verses 3–5a. Does this mean Paul is praying all day and all night for the Christians at Colossae? Probably not. It's more likely that Paul has regular prayer hours, perhaps morning and evening, and he always includes this church in those prayer times.

Notice the trifecta of faith, hope, and love in these verses. Paul often includes these three essentials of the Christian life in his writings. These are the basics, the fundamentals that form a sort of litmus test for an authentic faith. He has heard that all three exist in the church at Colossae. Notice how they work together. These brothers and sisters have a hope that is stored up or reserved for them in heaven. What is it that is reserved? God himself, the presence of Jesus, and intimacy with him. This hope is not speaking of an inward disposition but rather of the object on which it rests. These saints know their future includes living forever with Christ in his joy. It is this hope that then produces their faith and love.

Think of it this way: perhaps you must spend several hours with a difficult person. Would it not dramatically affect your ability to love that person if you knew that what followed those few hours would be a wonderfully planned afternoon with your best friend? The hope of that joy would certainly seep into the morning hours and transform your behavior. This is the same hope we hold as believers. We have the certain expectation of spending eternity with Christ in a place of peace and joy. As this knowledge settles into our hearts, it increases our faith and love for our brothers and sisters now.

Verses 5b–6. "The word of truth" in 5b could easily be translated "for what it truly is." In other words, Paul is telling the Colossian believers that in the past they have heard the good news of the gospel for what it truly is. Here we get some of the first hints of why Paul is writing his letter. While the false teachers in their midst had been telling them they needed something more or something deeper than Christ, Paul begins to explain that the gospel they first heard was the real deal, the truth, sufficient. The gospel came to Colossae and began to effect change, just as it had in other parts of the world. Its work authenticates its power.

Paul is not necessarily referring to every square inch of the earth when he refers to the "whole world." He means that just as God intended for Israel to be a banner of God's goodness to the entire ancient world, so the gospel had begun to infiltrate every people group outside of the Jewish nation. In verse 6, "bearing fruit and increasing" is a clear reference to the creation mandate given to humanity. In Genesis 1:28 God told Adam and Eve, "Be fruitful and multiply and fill the earth." Adam failed to carry out his responsibilities when he sinned. Paul is explaining that this gospel that had spread to Colossae was doing what Adam failed to do—bearing fruit and increasing. What began as a mission to reproduce new image-bearers and to cultivate the fruitfulness of the garden of Eden now finds its fullest expression in the spiritual fruit that the Holy Spirit produces in those who believe in Jesus. Because we are in Christ, we are a part of the fruit bearing of the gospel. As N.T. Wright states, "In Christ there is a new beginning, a new Genesis."[1] What an immense privilege and pleasure.

Verses 7-8. Here we learn the name of the one who first carried the good news to the Colossians: Epaphras. It is likely that Epaphras had come to Ephesus when Paul was ministering there between 53 and 55 AD (see Acts 19:10), heard the gospel, and returned home to Colossae to spread the news and begin a church that eventually met in Philemon's home. Paul had not met these brothers and sisters but had been filled in on their faith and troubles by Epaphras. Out of love and concern for his fellow believers, he then traveled to Paul during one of

---

[1] Wright, *Colossians*, 60.

his prison stays in order to describe the false teaching that was infiltrating the church and ask for help in how to combat it. The letter we read today was Paul's response.

Paul may not have known the individuals at Colossae, but he knew one thing was true for each of them, just as it is for us: Christ is sufficient. The work Jesus did in his life, death, resurrection, and ascension is all we need to have peace with God. His obedience we now count as our obedience if we are in Christ. Our spiritual lives may be full and satisfying because of him. When we see the gospel for what it really is, we understand this foundational truth: Christ is sufficient.

Reflection Questions

4. Paul wrote the greeting of his letters in the format of the day, changing parts to reflect gospel truth. Can you think of cultural norms that Christians have subtly changed in this way?

5. Paul used the word "saints" to describe the believers at Colossae, but that word applies to us as well. This is more about our standing with God and less about our behavior. Is this an easy word to call yourself? Why or why not?

6. Colossian believers had a hope that impacted their day to day because of the object upon which their hope rested, heaven with the Lord. How often does this hope shape your day? How could leaning into this thought make an impact?

7. Verse 6 is a nod to Genesis 1:28 and the command given to Adam and Eve, but in this context it references being fruitful as spreading the gospel. How does this bring a deeper understanding of that original mandate than you had before?

8. Epaphras, the minister at Colossae, is caring deeply for his flock by seeking the counsel and guidance of Paul for issues in his church. When have you seen your pastor do this? How has it been helpful?

Focus verse: *We always thank God, the Father of our Lord Jesus Christ, when we pray for you, since we heard of your faith in Christ Jesus and of the love that you have for all the saints.*
Colossians 1:3-4

Reflections, curiosities, frustrations:

Study 3

Strengthened with All Power

Read Colossians 1:9–14

Observation Questions

1. What specific things was Paul praying for the church at Colossae in verses 9-10?

2. Rewrite verses 11-12 in your own words.

3. According to verses 13-14, what things has Jesus done for the believer?

Interpretation

In the first section of his letter, Paul introduces himself to this mostly Gentile church of fairly new believers, assuring them that the gospel they learned from Epaphras was what had borne fruit in them, just as it had around the world. Paul will now explain to the Colossians his regular prayer for them, which centers on Jesus, the one sufficient to redeem them and us.

Verses 9–10. "And so" refers to Paul's comments in verses 3–8. He knows that the gospel has been producing fruit in the Colossian church. What is the fruit being borne by these believers? They are doing good works and increasing in their knowledge of God. "And so" from the day Paul, Timothy, and other believers heard about this church, they've been praying regularly for them. The fruit borne in this little church is evidence of God's work in them, which emboldens Paul to ask for more. Demonstrations of God's power can do the same for us. Any fruit we see in ourselves or others should energize our prayers to the one who always initiates growth and fruit.

For what do Paul and his ministry partners pray so regularly? Notice the category in which they pray: the eternal. It is not that Paul and his friends do not care about worldly circumstances, but Paul sees that, as Sinclair Ferguson has said, "the practical needs of these believers can only be met out of the riches of their fellowship with and knowledge of Jesus."[1] When we only pray for the alleviation of circumstances, we ask for too little from our powerful God. And so Paul prays big prayers.

Paul asks for knowledge of God's will in order to walk in a manner worthy of him. We might read these words and think Paul is asking that they might know what specific plans or

---

[1] Ferguson, "Solid Joys."

decisions God wanted them to make. Instead, Paul is asking that they might understand God's desire to save them through Christ; this is his ultimate will. Paul wants them to be filled with the knowledge of God, so much so that their understanding of what God wants begins to characterize them as people. He prays for them a profound awareness of who God is and what his character means for the world. He prays that they will deeply know Jesus.

Again we see Paul using Old Testament allusions as he speaks of being "filled" in verse 9. Just as God "filled" certain Israelites with the Spirit in order that they might build beautiful pieces of the tabernacle way back in the time of Moses (see Exodus 31), so now Paul asks that God would "fill" believers with such an awareness of God and his will that they might build beautiful moral lives.[2] Notice that walking in this manner enables believers to be "fully pleasing to him." Of course these brothers and sisters who love Jesus want to please him. Paul is about to tell them and us how to do so.

Paul uses four words in the Greek that describe a "walk," or lifestyle, that pleases God (all -ing words): bearing fruit, growing in knowledge of God, being strengthened with God's power, and giving thanks. The first and second are found in verse 10. How might they live a life that fully pleases God? Bear fruit and grow in knowledge of him. This is again a clear reference to Genesis 1:28, where God commissioned Adam and Eve to be fruitful and multiply. The Colossians were to bear spiritual fruit and multiply in their understanding of God and his desires and will. Part of living a life that brings honor and glory to God is walking day by day in a way that realizes and values the reality of who Jesus is. His place in the life of a believer shapes all else. Again, this is not just intellectual assent but a wholehearted trust and reliance that submits itself to

---

[2] Beale, *Colossians*, 55.

Jesus as the master of one's life, owner of all things, and goal of every endeavor.

Verses 11-12. Verse 11 contains the third part of a walk that pleases God: "being strengthened with all power, according to his glorious might." Bearing fruit and growing in knowledge of God in order to please him are never things believers do on their own. While we do put forth effort, it is only in response to the power that God gives. The strength of the believer comes from God. This is not a license to "let go and let God," abdicate our responsibility, and hope that fruit and growth happen. Instead, this is an encouragement for the Colossians and all believers to trust and obey God's law of love knowing that his strength will be our strength.

Douglas Moo paraphrases verse 11, "strengthened by God with the greatest strength imaginable."[3] When we feel weary of doing good, frustrated and disheartened by suffering or false teaching around us like these Colossians, what God promises is that we do not need to survive by scraping by with our own flimsy, waffling, wavering strength. We also do not need to look to outside rituals or rules, as the Colossians may have been tempted to do by the false teachers in their midst. Instead, God will give us his own strength through the Spirit, the strength that raised Jesus from the dead and fashioned the mountains and seas. This is the strength offered to us in Christ. Our growth in the knowledge of Jesus and his will goes along with this strength, bolstering our ability to endure all circumstances. God enables us by his power to endure hardship, pain, and all kinds of suffering. By his power he gives us patience to endure terrible pressure and long waits. As we grow in our understanding and awe of Jesus's power, love, and sufficiency, our ability to keep all other things in our life in perspective grows. This kind of patience and even joy in suffering is only ever possible by God's power.

---

[3] Moo, *Letters*, 97.

Verse 12 includes the fourth part of a walk that pleases God: "giving thanks." For what should the Colossians give thanks? The Father has qualified these believers to share in the inheritance, literally the "lot" of the saints. It was not their behavior that earned them their portion in this life and a guarantee of eternal blessings after death. Rather, God made them worthy by his work. Just as the Israelites looked forward to their inheritance—the Promised Land—not because of their work but because of God's rescue, so even the Gentile Colossians and we now anticipate our inheritance of eternal rest because Jesus's work makes us worthy of it.

Verses 13-14. Though not specifically named in these verses, Paul references exodus ideas in this section. The Exodus of Israel out of Egypt is *the* major Old Testament paradigm for God's work of rescue. His sinful people were trapped in a place of darkness, in bondage to the Egyptian taskmasters, unable to liberate themselves; they were in need of God's powerful, sufficient, and effective love to redeem them from slavery. God sent a rescuer (Moses) to bring them out of Egypt and into a physical place promised to them, all at his (God's) own initiative and desire. In the same way, the sinful Colossians and all people were trapped in the "domain of darkness." We were born in sin, under the active authority of Satan and in his kingdom, unable to rescue ourselves from the bondage of our sin. When applied to our lives through faith, Jesus's righteous life, death, resurrection, and ascension transfer us from the kingdom of darkness to the kingdom of light. This is the kingdom of God, governed by the Son who is loved by his Father. In Christ the Gentiles and Jews in Colossae were promised a place of rest in the future, just as Israelites were given the promise of Canaan. This spiritual rescue worked by Jesus is just as real and secure as the physical rescue worked by God in the Exodus. It is his power and initiative that redeems us from the slavery of sin and the kingdom of darkness and transfers us to his own kingdom of light.

The word translated "redemption" in verse 14 expresses a release from some type of debt or bondage. We were in debt and bondage to sin. Jesus paid that debt and released us. When the Colossians heard this word, they would have immediately thought of the price paid to release a slave from slavery in their first-century context. Here we learn that in Christ, we are redeemed, purchased, and released from our slavery to sin. His work is sufficient to make us free.

Paul and his friends with him heard about the believers at Colossae and immediately began to pray for them. They prayed that these men and women would know God in order to walk in a way that pleased him, bearing fruit, growing in knowledge of him, being strengthened by him, and giving thanks. We can pray for ourselves and others in the same way. Jesus has already bought our freedom from sin, transferred us from the kingdom of Satan to his own, and promised us an inheritance of endless joy with him. His work and obedience on our behalf is sufficient to enable us to live lives that please him. His love is sufficient to satisfy us. His power is sufficient to transfer us from the domain of darkness into his light.

Reflection Questions

4. Paul prays big prayers asking for deep spiritual truths to be applied to the life of a believer. Do you ever pray this way? Why or why not?

5. Paul describes a life walking in a "manner worthy of the Lord" as one that is bearing fruit, growing in knowledge of God, being empowered by the Holy Spirit, and giving thanks. Give practical examples of what each of these things look like.

6. After Paul lists the things he is praying for, he goes on to tell the Colossian believers the means by which they will occur in them: the strength of God's power. When you are wanting a heart change in yourself, do you ask God's power to be the source? What do you rely on instead?

7. How does reflecting on the Exodus narrative help you understand the freedom you have been given through Jesus and God's rescue of you? What about this do you think was helpful for the Colossians to hear?

8. Paul prays for four spiritual truths to show up in the lives of the Colossians: bearing fruit, growing in knowledge of God, being strengthened with God's power, and giving thanks. Which one do you want to pray for yourself? Which one do you want to pray for someone you love? Write a prayer.

Focus verse: *Being strengthened with all power, according to his glorious might, for all endurance and patience with joy.*
Colossians 1:11

Reflections, curiosities, frustrations:

Study 4

In Him All Things Hold Together

Read Colossians 1:15–23

Observation Questions

1. How does verse 15 describe Christ? What do verses 16-17 say Christ has authority over?

2. According to verses 18-19, who is Christ for the church? What does verse 20 say he will reconcile, where, and by what means?

3. What do verses 21-22 say about us as believers? What does verse 23 call us to do?

Interpretation

Having explained his regular prayer for the Colossians, Paul will now give them an incredible description of the supremacy of Christ. Colossians 1:15-20 is often called the "Colossian Hymn." We cannot be sure if believers sang these words in this exact sequence or if Paul borrowed some words from a well-known poem and added some to make his point. What is abundantly clear is that this is one of the most beautiful, most compelling passages of divine Christology in the Bible. In this soaring passage, Paul presents Christ as completely sufficient to reconcile us to God and rule all things.

Verses 15-16. Although a new sentence has begun, Paul is speaking of the same person he left off with in verse 14, the one "in whom we have redemption, the forgiveness of sins." Who is this who forgives? This is the beloved Son (verse 14), the image, likeness, or representation of the invisible God. This is another touchback to Genesis, where Adam and Eve were created in the image of God, or "according to his likeness." If we ever wonder who God is, what he might seem like up close, or what his character would be like if we could have a conversation with him, we only need to look at Jesus. He is the visible representation of the Father's personality and nature.

Jesus is also the firstborn, which could lead us to believe Paul means he is a created being instead of an eternal one. However, the word "firstborn" here has a metaphorical meaning. In ancient cultures this referred sometimes to birth order but more importantly to elevation or standing in a social system or family. Jesus is the highest, the greatest, the foremost of all creation. We are sure of this because of what Paul tells us next.

Jesus is the agent or power by which all things were created, and therefore he rules over them. When we consider what he created, we must not only think of the katydids and kangaroos, the volcanoes and velociraptors. Paul purposely uses the word "all" seven times in these first six verses so that we might understand the scope of Jesus's authority. Included are animate and inanimate things, visible and invisible things. From hairy mountain goats to color changing octopuses, from deep ocean trenches to snow covered mountain ranges, all are governed by Jesus. But also all things in the spiritual realm, whether evil or good, are under his rule and reign. All angelic beings, demons, evil powers, and unseen forces ultimately are ruled by Jesus. Paul wants these believers to know that whatever forces are at work in their everyday lives, whatever evil powers or authorities are exerting pressure, causing struggle, or working to hurt or destroy them are "unable to rival Christ in any way."[1] This would have been extremely important given the false teaching in the Colossian church that said more than the gospel was needed for spiritual fullness. Paul plainly states that no power can overcome Jesus. Every object, person, authority, and place was created through him and for him. He is the beginning of all and the goal of all.

Verses 17–18. Jesus is before all things in the sense that he existed before anything was created. He is the eternal God. And just as all things were created through him and by him, so now all things hold together by his power. The entire universe—every molecule of water and blowfish, every planet's orbit and gravitational plane, every pericardial sac and pair of lungs, everything and everyone is held together by Christ and his power.

---

[1] Moo, *Letters*, 123.

Apparently some of the false teachers were suggesting that believers needed to find sources in addition to Christ to find fullness in their spiritual life. Paul tells them here that Christ is the head of the body, meaning the ruler and life-giver to his body, the church. There is no other point of supply. But even more than that, Jesus is the firstborn from the dead. When he rose from the dead after his crucifixion, he began a new order, a new kind of humanity, of whom he is the first. Paul expects many brothers and sisters to follow in Christ's footsteps, to be resurrected and join this new kind of people.

Unlike the false teachers who tried to convince the Colossians that they must add ritual, rules, or experience to Christ and his salvation, Paul tells them that Jesus is preeminent, meaning superior and peerless. He is all that is needed to know God and experience God. Just as he is in charge of humanity and the earth's creatures in our present age, so he will be the unequaled leader of the new resurrected humanity in the age to come. His sovereignty is not dependent upon the acknowledgement of those he rules. He is their unrivaled chief, no matter their posture toward him.

Verses 19–20. In other words, God with all of his power, glory, energy, holiness, and compassion has chosen to reside in Jesus. All of God can be found in him. While the false teachers may have been teaching that spiritual fullness and satisfaction was available in some combination of Jesus plus their own rigid activity schedule, Paul asserts that true fullness, the fullness of who God is, can only be found in Christ. While in the Old Testament God chose to dwell in the tabernacle to be near his people, now he has chosen to dwell through the person of Jesus with his people—the church. Just as the temple was the place to sacrifice animals and their blood in order to atone for sin and be reconciled to God, so now Jesus's blood reconciles all things to God. This does not prove universalism, the belief that all people will be saved. This would be in direct opposition to so much of Paul's and Jesus's teaching. Instead, the Father has initiated through his Son the process of making peace with humanity. Just as all things were cursed because of humanity's rebellion against God, so all things will be reconciled because of Jesus's sacrifice.

Verses 21–23. These three verses are all one long sentence. Douglas Moo tells us the bare bones of the sentence are ". . . you . . . he reconciled . . . to present you . . . if you continue."[2] What does Paul say about the Colossians before Christ? They were hostile to God in their minds, which led to evil behavior. We are all in this position without the work of Jesus. God took the initiative to reconcile sinners to himself by sending Jesus, who took on flesh, a physical body, and died. When applied to humans, his death achieves for us the status of being faultless and blameless. This means that if we are in Christ, every fault, blame, large sin, and small misdemeanor has been atoned for in Christ.

The phrase "to present you" tells us Paul is referring to the final judgment. Just as the high priest would present the sacrificial lamb as an offering for atonement, so Christ offers himself as the lamb, which reconciles these believers to God. Verse 23 reads as a warning, but an extremely pastoral one. Paul is concerned that these believers will listen to those speaking lies into their ears that say hope in Jesus is not enough, that something else must be added. He does not want them to shift from the hope of the gospel or strive to add something to the gospel to be saved or fully experience God.

It may seem a small thing to add little bits to the gospel. If the Colossians had the core understanding that Jesus died for their sins, why did the rest matter? It mattered to Epaphras and to Paul, and it matters to us because if Jesus and his work is not everything we rely on for the good life, for true satisfaction, for a full spirituality, then he is nothing. Only Jesus and his work is sufficient to save and fulfill us. Only Jesus himself will get the glory for our salvation.

---

[2] Ibid., 139.

Reflection Questions

4. Paul wants these believers to know that no force in heaven or earth can rival Christ and his authority. What comforts you most about this truth? What about this truth makes you uneasy?

5. All things were not just created through Christ but are held together by him. This is just one of many descriptions of Christ's supremacy in this letter. What about the scope of this is a new thought for you?

6. All of who God is resides in Jesus. Have you viewed God and Jesus as different? How does this reshape your view of each of them?

7. Without Christ's intervention in our lives, we are hostile toward God, which leads to evil behavior. Is this how you have viewed yourself before you became a Christian (no matter at what age that was)? Why or why not?

8. Paul is showing concern that these believers are trying to add something to Jesus's supremacy, causing them not to see Christ as sufficient. In what ways has the authority and supremacy of Christ not felt like enough to you? What do you need to repent of?

Focus verse: *And he is before all things, and in him all things hold together. And he is the head of the body, the church. He is the beginning, the firstborn from the dead, that in everything he might be preeminent.*
Colossians 1:17–18

Reflections, curiosities, frustrations:

Study 5

God's Mystery

Read Colossians 1:24–2:5

Observation Questions

1. According to chapter 1, verses 24–25 and 28–29, and chapter 2, verses 4–5, what is Paul doing and why?

2. Chapter 1, verses 26–27 use the word "mystery" twice. Define "mystery." What is the mystery according to the text?

3. In chapter 2, verses 2-3, Paul tells them he is writing this to them in hopes that what things will happen?

Interpretation

In the last study, we saw the preeminence of Christ in the soaring hymn of chapter 1, verses 15-20, along with Paul's hope that the Colossians would continue in the faith. There is a distinct shift in chapter 1, verse 24, as Paul begins to talk about his own ministry. "Struggle" is a frequent word in these verses. For any who follow Jesus, and especially for those who minister in his name, struggle will be a part of everyday life. Just as the shape of Jesus's life was that of crucifixion and resurrection, death then life, so the lives of his followers will always include death and life, struggle and hope.

Chapter 1, verses 24–26. Verse 24 can be confusing at first. Is Paul saying that because Jesus didn't suffer enough, he is finishing the job? Christ's suffering was in no way inadequate. Paul seems to be saying that what has not yet been "filled up" is the suffering or affliction that must happen alongside Paul's gospel ministry in the world. Paul is going to have to suffer while he is doing ministry. Jesus said this very thing about Paul in Acts 9:16 as he spoke to Ananias, "For I will show him how much he must suffer for the sake of my name." Suffering in some way seems to be the norm for those who spread the message of the gospel. To differentiate Jesus's sufferings from ours, J.B. Lightfoot uses the terms "satisfactory" (Christ's sufferings) and "ministerial" (those endured in ministry).[1] Meaning, Jesus suffered for our sin on the cross in a way that satisfied God's justice and righteousness. This is satisfactory suffering. Then, Paul suffers and we suffer for the sake of the gospel. This is ministerial suffering. Though Paul is emphasizing his own afflictions, all believers have an allotted portion of suffering. As Jesus said in John 15:20, "Remember the word that I said to you: 'A servant is not greater than his master. If they persecuted me, they will also persecute you.'"

In verse 25, the word "stewardship" in the ESV or "commission" in the NIV is sometimes associated with a specific job or responsibility. Paul's specific commission from God was to bring the gospel to the Gentiles, the non-Jews, which most of the Colossians were. Paul was to make God's word fully known to his saints, including the mystery that was not known for hundreds of years previously. This mystery was not hidden or buried, but it was only partially understood in the age of the Old Testament. The plan of God to save all nations was always in place but was only fully revealed in the life, death, and resurrection of Jesus. This word "mystery" probably comes from Daniel 2, where King Nebuchadnezzar's dream is a mystery. The broad and sweeping plan of salvation for both Jews and Gentiles was made known by Paul in his ministry.

Chapter 1, verses 27–29. God has made his plan for redemption known to his saints, the church. We take this for granted; it is so familiar to us. But remember, for hundreds of years and many generations, the Jewish nation was God's chosen people with whom he made a covenant. To be redeemed one had to be connected to Israel. There were hints in the Old Testament of God's love for the nations but nothing as overt as the

---

[1] As quoted by Moo, *Letters*, 151.

proclamation of God's love and plan that included non-Jews. Most of us would have been outsiders to God's people. Now God was revealing his plan to the Gentiles. Unlike the "mystery religions" of the day that required some sort of special revelation from God or extra ritual to be saved, the true mystery of God has been revealed for all: it is Christ. Because we are connected to him and he is in us, we have the hope of glory, the hope not only of being saved but of seeing the fullness of God's glory in the new heavens and earth.

And so Paul and his companions proclaim Jesus, warning and teaching everyone as they explain the mystery of Christ. These tasks of warning and teaching include both believers and unbelievers, as their goal is to present everyone "mature in Christ." Some translations use the word "perfect" instead of "mature." We in the West often understand "perfect" to mean flawless or accurate, but that is not the sense here; Paul's aim is to present everyone as fully formed, ready for the end, mature in Christ. Paul wants each believer to stand before God on the final day with a heart that is completely committed to him. This happens, Paul believes, through teaching Christ and also warning about distractions from Christ's ability to save. It is easy to forget the goal as we labor on every day, meeting deadlines, caring for children, friends, or parents, paying bills, and cooking meals. The goal of our lives is not money, safety, obedient children, health, or an excellent work record, though all of those are good things. The goal as Paul speaks of it in Colossians is to walk in a manner worthy of the Lord, and please him in every way (Colossians 1:10). This is the maturity of which Paul writes.

In order that he may present these believers mature in Christ, Paul labors and strains, struggling with God's power and ability that works in him. This is always the tension for those in ministry and all believers. We work. We strive. We struggle against temptation and discouragement, disappointment when others leave the faith, frustration at setbacks, and our general weakness. But we do not fight with our own strength. We do not work by our own power. We are energized, empowered, and enabled by Jesus himself to struggle and to serve.

Chapter 2, verses 1–3. Though he has never met them, Paul struggles in prayer for the believers at Colossae and Laodicea, which was about nine miles from Colossae. He prays in particular against the false teachings about which Epaphras informed him, and that their hearts might be encouraged. Paul is not hoping for a purely emotional outcome. "Heart" here is the core of a person's connection to God. It is not separate from the mind and will. Paul is praying that as they know Christ's sufficiency, it will translate into actions of love for one another. As they are more and more confident in their salvation, which is secure and achieved by Christ alone, he prays they will move toward unity as believers.

Paul wants the Colossians to know that everything they need can be found in Christ. Unlike the false teaching that tells these brothers and sisters to supplement Jesus with man made rules that have the appearance of wisdom and knowledge, Paul wants them to know that real wisdom and knowledge, which are relevant, valued, and helpful, can be found only in Christ. These treasures are not hidden in the sense that they cannot be found but that they have been stored up in Jesus, kept safe, deposited. While the Old Testament studied wisdom from a variety of different angles, that wisdom is now fully revealed in one person: Jesus Christ. Over and over Paul repeats the sufficiency of Christ in opposition to the claims of the false teachers.

Chapter 2, verses 4–5. The arguments being used to try to convince the Colossians of Christ plus some rules or rituals for fullness must have sounded quite convincing or plausible. Paul was writing about Christ's sufficiency and authority in order that these saints would not be misguided or duped by false teaching. Paul could not physically be in the same space, but his spirit was with them in the sense that the Holy Spirit connects all believers.

Verse 5 tells us that the Colossians had not succumbed to the false teaching, as Paul rejoices in their good order and firmness in their faith. By "order" he probably means not physical orderliness but the good order of their doctrine, a clear understanding of the gospel alone. Their faith was firm, not wavering or doubting at this point. As Walter Wink writes, "The epistle is a vaccination against heresy, not an antibiotic for those already afflicted."[2]

At the time of Paul's writing, these brothers and sisters apparently still had a good understanding of the gospel, the hope in Christ's work alone for their salvation. But some false teachers, we don't know how many, had begun to penetrate the church community, attempting to convince them they needed to add some sort of practice to the gospel to be spiritually satisfied or to go to the "next level" in their faith. Paul is determined to convince them that they have all that is necessary, and they have it in the church. Jesus is now dwelling in them; the fullness of God is among his people. They do not need to go elsewhere to find all of God's presence and satisfaction.

We are not immune to this type of teaching. Though it may not be Jewish ritual or some sort of man-made rule-keeping, we may believe it is Jesus plus a specific spiritual practice, Jesus plus the right conference or teacher, Jesus plus the right therapist, or Jesus plus correct doctrine that will satisfy us. But Christ alone is sufficient. Christ is the mystery, the treasure, the goal. Christ is sufficient to save us and to grow us to maturity as he works among his people, the church.

---

[2] As quoted in ibid., 175.

Reflection Questions

4. Suffering is something all believers will experience, even as they minister in Jesus's name. What about this is confusing to you? What about this makes sense?

5. This mystery, which was to save God's people through the death and resurrection of Jesus, was only partially understood by believers before Christ came. We, on the other hand, have always lived with this mystery revealed to us. How does that deepen our understanding? What should we do with that knowledge?

6. The goal of Paul's teaching and warning about false views of the gospel was to make them fully formed, ready to stand before God on the final day with a heart that is committed to him—which is the definition of being mature in Christ. How does this add to your understanding of maturity in Christ? What does this make you long to grow in?

7. Paul is praying that they will know deep in their heart that Christ is completely sufficient for them and in him are hidden all the treasures of knowledge and insight that they need. What kind of impact could a prayer like this have had on their struggles? What impact could it have on your current struggles?

8. Paul was struggling to prepare them for and protect them from a philosophy that had not fully taken hold yet. What does this show us about proactive versus reactive teaching? How could this approach be beneficial in current Christian circles you are a part of?

Focus verse: *That their hearts may be encouraged, being knit together in love, to reach all the riches of full assurance of understanding and the knowledge of God's mystery, which is Christ, in whom are hidden all the treasures of wisdom and knowledge.*
Colossians 2:2–3

Reflections, curiosities, frustrations:

Study 6

Together with Him

Read Colossians 2:6–15

Observation Questions

1. What is Paul encouraging the Colossians to do in verses 6-7?

2. What does verse 8 warn against?

3. List all the things Christ did for you according to verses 11-15.

Interpretation

Paul explained in the last passage that he was glad to suffer for the Colossians, so that they might deeply know Jesus and become mature in him. He explained Jesus's preeminence and that all wisdom and treasure is found in Christ. Given the power of God and the fullness of provision the Colossians have in Jesus, Paul now issues them his first command. This is the center of the book, the right response to all that Jesus has done for them: "as you received Christ Jesus the Lord, so walk in him."

Verses 6-7. Notice that Paul has written an entire chapter (though chapters would not have been divided in the original letter) to these dear brothers and sisters before issuing a single command. He wants them to understand how they've been loved, given the fullness of God in Christ, and how he has willingly prayed and struggled for them before he ever asks for a response. This must always be the order for those of us who want to follow Jesus. First we receive from him; then we respond to him. First we are loved by him; then we walk in obedience. We must never reverse this order and attempt to earn his love by our actions. Our walk does not earn grace but expresses the grace we've been given.

In naming "Christ Jesus the Lord," Paul is probably repeating the early Christian confession "Jesus is Lord." Receiving Jesus meant receiving his teaching as well. Walking in him meant living according to his Word. The Colossians' lives had to be centered on Christ's supremacy. Their conduct had to be governed by his ethics. But how could they walk in this way? Only by being rooted in Christ, built up in Christ, established in the faith, and abounding in thanksgiving.

Just as Paul gave us four participles (-ing words) that defined what it meant to walk in a manner worthy of Jesus in chapter 1, verses 10–12, so here Paul gives four more words that show the Colossians and us how to center our lives on Jesus. We root ourselves in Christ so that he might provide all the nourishment and strength we need to grow. We are built up in him as he grows us and sanctifies us. As we stay rooted in him, God establishes us or firms up our faith. As we learn to rely on him, our hearts overflow with thanksgiving. Our bond with Jesus is the life-giving connection that allows us to "walk in him." This way of life is impossible unless we are rooted in him.

Verses 8–10. Paul warns in verse 8 against being carried off by false teaching like a person being carried off as a captive of war. Paul had no problem with philosophy as a discipline. He was opposed to systems of thought that were "not according to Christ" and that gave some other answer to life's ultimate problems. For the Colossians this probably included gods or spirits that required the performance of certain rituals to reach spiritual fulfillment. Paul argued that the Christian believers already had what they needed for the fullest possible experience spiritually—the fullness of God himself. As God dwelt in the temple of Israel, so he dwelt in Christ and now dwells in the church. The one who is "the head of all rule and authority" had revealed himself completely in his church. God, who rules all of the spiritual world, was among them. What else could they possibly need? We, like these Colossians, may be enticed by gurus or popular teachers who promise the next level of spiritual or emotional experience if we would just listen to them. We must hear the warning to remain rooted in Christ alone.

Verses 11–12. Why is Paul suddenly writing to a mostly Gentile church about circumcision, a Jewish tradition? Circumcision for Israel was a physical action performed by a priest that signified one's belonging to the people of God, being set apart for God, and depending on him and his covenant promises. Circumcision of the heart is a spiritual action performed by the Holy Spirit that signifies one's belonging to the church, being set apart for God, and depending on Christ and his promises for salvation. It involves a cutting off from the sinful world and the flesh's temptations.

In verse 12, Paul continues his explanation of the changes that occur when someone is transferred to Christ's kingdom. When a person comes to Christ, their old self or their old slavery to sin and death is buried and a new life begins. When we are united to Christ, the death and new life of Jesus become ours. Baptism is just the outward picture of how this happens in our souls. This is a mysterious and amazing bond for the believer in Christ. Romans 6:3-4 elaborates on this incredible death to life movement as Paul writes, "Do you not know that all of us who have been baptized into Christ Jesus were baptized into his death? We were buried therefore with him by baptism into death, in order that, just as Christ was raised from the dead by the glory of the Father, we too might walk in newness of life." Being united with Jesus through faith means that we spiritually died and have been raised with him.

Paul goes on in Romans 6:5-8: "For if we have been united with him in a death like his, we shall certainly be united with him in a resurrection like his. We know that our old self was crucified with him in order that the body of sin might be brought to nothing, so that we would no longer be enslaved to sin. For one who has died has been set free from sin. Now if we have died with Christ, we believe that we will also live with him." Our old life of sin has been buried, though we still are tempted and struggle against it. But we "will also live with him." That is, we will be raised to life physically just as Jesus was. This rising from the dead has already begun in us, as we have been spiritually raised already. All of this is the fruit of our union with Christ.

Verses 13–15. Before belonging to Christ, these believers were dead, slaves to their sinful nature, and unable to obey God. It is not the case that every human can choose whether to obey at any given moment and that Christians just obey more of the time. Humans cannot obey God until they are given a new heart, made alive. Once God makes us alive with Jesus, the choice to respond to his love with obedience becomes a reality in our lives.

But how did God make us alive? In an astounding and fascinating way. In verse 14, Paul explains a sort of document that lists all of the ways we should act in our loyalty or devotion to God, a sort of IOU that we both wrote and signed. This document indicts us because of our clear and daily failure to obey his will completely. But instead of punishing us, God canceled or wiped away our debt. Not only that, he took the very paper it was written on and nailed it to the cross. God made us alive by both forgiving our sin and paying for the IOU himself. In theological terms, this is penal substitution. Christ was punished in our place, satisfying the demands of God's justice.

This canceling of the debt of sinners had ramifications for more than the humans it benefitted. The rulers and authorities, meaning the servants of Satan and spiritual beings opposed to God and his kingdom, were disarmed in this transaction. The picture here is that of a commander of armies who has won a battle, stripped his enemies of their weapons and armor, and parades them through town in an exposing and shaming victory parade that ends in their death. Sin and Satan therefore have no power over these Colossian believers. Though Satan continues to tempt and discourage, whisper lies to and distract believers, his actual power over them was lost when Jesus nailed their debt to his cross.

What more could we seek? This is what has been done for us. This is what is ours if we are in Christ. No human political system, strategic plan, religious ritual, or spiritual practice could ever offer this level of satisfaction, this full of a salvation, this sure triumph over death. Only Christ's death and resurrection are sufficient to save. Only Christ's power is sufficient to conquer death. Only Christ, who now dwells in his people, in his church, is sufficient to make us alive again.

Reflection Questions

4. Paul's call to the Colossians starts with the reminder that first they received Christ, then they walk in him, not the other way around. Why do we want to reverse this order? What happens if we do reverse it?

5. Paul gives four descriptors of what flows out of a life joined with Christ (verses 6–7). Of those four, which do you see the most in yourself? Which do you see the least? What can you pray for?

6. The Colossians had been enticed by the idea that another level of spiritual fulfillment, beyond what they found in Christ, was obtainable if they added certain ways of thinking and physical practices. When have you been tempted to think in a similar way? What made this appealing to you at the time?

7. Paul details all the things that happen to believers that are united with Christ: they experience a circumcision of the heart, die with Christ, are raised to life with him, and have all their debt against them canceled (verses 12–15). Which of these things are you most in awe of? Why?

8. Not only were sinners' debts canceled by Christ, but Satan's servants were also disarmed by Jesus's work on the cross. This leaves Satan only able to tempt, discourage, or lie to believers but not have power over them. How does this change your understanding of the limitations of Satan's schemes against you?

Focus verse: *See to it that no one takes you captive by philosophy and empty deceit, according to human tradition, according to the elemental spirits of the world, and not according to Christ. For in him the whole fullness of deity dwells bodily, and you have been filled in him, who is the head of all rule and authority.*
Colossians 2:8-10

Reflections, curiosities, frustrations:

Study 7

Read Colossians 2:16-3:4

Observation Questions

1. In chapter 2, verses 16 and 18, what things did Paul say not to let others pass judgment or disqualify them for?

2. Summarize what point you think Paul is making in chapter 2, verses 20–23.

3. According to chapter 3, verses 1–4, where is Christ? What are the specific things that happen to believers due to Christ's death?

Interpretation

Paul spent ample time explaining to the Colossians that they must hold onto the truth of Christ instead of empty teachings. He reminded them that they had been buried with Jesus in their baptism and made alive with him, had been forgiven of their sins, and were free from the debt they owed God because of their union with Jesus. Paul will speak specifically in this section about the claims of these false teachers and how to behave in light of them.

Chapter 2, verses 16–19. Apparently these false teachers were condemning the Colossian Christians for not following certain Old Testament food laws, referred to in the phrase "food and drink," and for not observing special days, indicated by the phrase "festival or a new moon or a Sabbath." All of these were put in place by God as a foreshadowing of the coming of Jesus. Food laws were observed to make oneself clean for worship in the temple. But only Jesus can make us ultimately clean and able to enter into worship of a holy God. Festivals and special days were observed to remember God's faithfulness and experience his presence in the temple. But Jesus became a man that we might experience God's presence in the flesh, and he now dwells in his people, the church.

Food and drink regulations and festivals were all a part of the time of promise. They were anticipatory, pointing to Christ, the goal. Christ had come, and in him these brothers and sisters had the fullness of God. Therefore, there was no reason to let anyone judge them as less than or in error for not observing old rules and practices. Here we get some specific descriptions of other activities the false teachers required to reach status as a "real" or "first class" Christian. They prescribed some sort of angel worship that demanded harsh treatment of the body to prepare for the experience. They would go on and on about their spiritual experience and visions, arrogantly holding their encounters with angels over the heads of those who hadn't had them.

These brothers in the church were not connected to Jesus, the head of the body, the church. The church is nourished, grows, and unites under its head, Christ. Without the head directing the body, this man-made religion had no source of growth, no heavenly connection, no real spiritual value.

Chapter 2, verses 20-23. Paul assumes the "if" portion of this statement is true. The Colossians were no longer in bondage to any other spiritual powers in the world. But they were acting as if they were, as if they had to submit to made up, worldly rules, when a fundamental break with the world had in fact taken place in them when they were united to Christ.

Paul is probably mocking the false teachers' general directives when he writes, "'Do not handle, Do not taste, Do not touch.'" These instructions most likely included not eating certain foods or drinking certain things as people prepared themselves physically for spiritual experiences. All of these directives were made-up procedures for a ritual or practice that was as temporary as the food and drink itself. These teachers may have seemed holy or wise in that they promoted asceticism, severe treatment of the body, but they weren't. They may have used these practices as a type of prevention of temptation, trying to control the body with harsh methods, all of which proved ineffective.

This false teaching obviously appealed to those who wanted to be sure they took their faith seriously, pushed it to the next level, and did everything within their control to get it right. But it was not according to Christ, and therefore it had no value. These practices had no power to bring real transformation, to change the heart or the mind, or to work salvation. Instead of being part of the supernatural work of Christ on behalf of believers to give them the fullness of God, this was a counterfeit avenue that only promised a spiritual experience. It did nothing to the heart to prepare these men and women to meet their holy God.

Chapter 3, verses 1–4. Having given these Colossians instructions on what not to do regarding the false teachers, Paul now gives them positive commands. These verses center on the believers' union with Christ, their solidarity and connection with Jesus that guarantees all of the benefits of salvation. Our union with Christ is how we, the branches, draw from Christ, the vine (John 15:5). We are linked to Jesus by our faith in this crucial and life-giving bond. Believers are to seek the things of heaven because that is where Jesus is. Though we must still live out our days on earth, we have already been "raised with Christ" spiritually.

Jesus is sitting, triumphant, at the right hand of the Father, having conquered sin and death. Those who are in Christ, fundamentally connected to him for their lives, have therefore also been raised. This is the already/not yet of Colossians. Paul is directing these believers to orient their lives to their spiritual reality and status—possessing all of the benefits of Christ's resurrection. As opposed to needing practices and rules in order to conquer their sin and flesh, these brothers and sisters have resurrection power to fight evil in themselves and in the world. As opposed to needing some extra experience of God brought on by harsh treatment of the body and visions of angels, they have all the experience of God they could ever need: they as the church are filled by God himself.

Believers are to make heavenly thoughts a habit, focusing on the riches we already have in Christ. We have died to this world and to the bondage of sin. Our lives are now bound up in Christ, "hidden" in the sense that they are "yet to be fully seen."[1] Because of him, we have forgiveness, protection from evil spirits, and the power to live in obedience and freedom. While we must walk through suffering, pain, and loss in the world like everyone else, we belong to another realm. Our spiritual identity is hidden but real. One day all will be revealed and our position will be made known to all, but, as Douglas Moo writes, "In the meantime, our true status is veiled."[2]

We wait for the day when Christ appears at the end of history. On that day he will be seen in his full majesty and beauty, the conquering king, our perfect savior. Though he is hidden now, he will be clearly seen by all. Those of us whose lives are hidden in him will appear with him, mature, without sin, having been completely transformed by his work. Everything, all of this, depends on our union with Christ. This is our hope; this is the future for which our hearts long and ache. We want to be made like him, to be with him, to be beyond the struggle against sin, the shaming voice of Satan, and the sufferings that whisper doubts to our souls. Dear believer, if you are in Christ, your day of glory with your Savior is guaranteed. Your appearance with Jesus in his blinding beauty and glory is as secure as Jesus's status at the right hand of the Father.

---

[1] Thompson, *Colossians*, 135.

[2] Moo, *Letters*, 250.

Reflection Questions

4. False teachers were telling the Colossian Christians to look beyond Christ and the normal means of grace—such as fellowship, communion, worship, and prayer—for a higher spiritual experience. When have you been led in a similar way of thinking? When have you passed that misguided thinking to others?

5. The Colossian Christians were no longer in bondage to spiritual powers in the world but were still living like they were. What do you think they hoped to gain by doing this? How can you relate to that?

6. We have union with Christ, which gives us the benefits of salvation(the hope of our own resurrection, power to fight evil, and connection to Jesus) in this very moment, in our daily lives. Which of these comforts you the most? Which do you long to experience more in your daily life?

7. You have died with Christ. You have been raised with him. What does it look like practically to orient your life to this spiritual reality and status?

8. "Our spiritual identity is hidden but real," and one day we will see it in fullness. What are you most excited to see or experience when that happens?

Focus verse: *If then you have been raised with Christ, seek the things that are above, where Christ is, seated at the right hand of God. Set your minds on things that are above, not on things that are on earth. For you have died, and your life is hidden with Christ in God. When Christ who is your life appears, then you also will appear with him in glory.*
Colossians 3:1-4

Reflections, curiosities, frustrations:

Study 8

Read Colossians 3:5–17

Observation Questions

1. List the things Paul says to "put to death" and "put them all away" in verses 5-9?

2. List the things Paul says to "put on" in verses 12-17?

3. Summarize what Paul is communicating in verses 10–11.

Interpretation

As you begin to study this portion of Colossians, keep in mind Paul's exhortation in chapter 3, verse 1: "If then you have been raised with Christ, seek the things that are above." Paul assumed that these brothers and sisters had been raised and therefore separated from their old lives of fleshly living. They were new people—not completely sin-free, but free from the dominance of sin, free to obey God, and a part of the new humanity God had begun when Jesus was resurrected. As new people in a new humanity, they must live according to their new identity.

Verses 5–7. Most translations render the first words of verse 5, "put to death." However, the NASB has made a helpful choice in translating, "Therefore, treat the parts of your earthly body as dead to sexual immorality." Believers are to act on the basis of the death that occurred in them; they are dead to the old man or old Adam—that is, to their old identity as one who was in the kingdom of Satan, bound by the chains of sin, and unable to obey God. Therefore, they should no longer act like spiritually dead people. This is the already/not yet of living as a saint who waits for our appearance with Jesus in glory. We have, like the Colossians, been made new. But temptations still surround us. As we grow in Christ over the years, we will make our old sin habits less and less of our present-day behavior.

This first list has the theme of sexual sin, which stems from unchecked desire. Paul tells us these sins are ultimately idolatry because desiring anything more than God is idolatry. It may be that new Gentile believers were generally prone to these types of sins. While vice lists (lists of behaviors that were to be avoided by citizens for the good of the whole community) were common in the New Testament world, their goal was usually the improvement of people's morals. Here Paul uses a vice list to detail behaviors and sinful desires that are characteristic of spiritually dead people in order to explain that God's wrath is imminent because of sin like this that breaks his moral law. Notice in verse 7 that Paul refers to this spiritually dead sin as something that was a regular part of the Colossians' past. This sin is what brought the wrath of God on to Christ on the cross. We must name this as sin and repent.

Verses 8-11. "But now" meaning "having been raised with Christ and now being alive in him," you must also stop doing the following things that affect your relationships in the church. The lies of the false teachers may have led some in the Colossian church to believe they were better than others because of their asceticism or harsh bodily practices. Paul mentions malice, which includes "a mean spirited or vicious attitude or disposition to someone."[1] Along with the rest of this list, these things combine to produce nasty, abusive speech toward one another, which destroys reputation and relationship.

Paul prohibits lying in verse 9 but quickly reminds the Colossian believers of how they might stop this behavior along with the others listed: "you have put off the old self with its practices and have put on the new self." The change has already happened, Paul tells them, so live accordingly. The old self belonged to Adam and his kind. The new self belongs to Christ

---

[1] Bauer, *Greek–English Lexicon*, 500.

71

and holds all of the privileges and benefits of Christ, including having died to that old way of life. Not only are believers a new creation, but God is continually renewing them to reflect the character of Jesus more and more. We are both "empowered and required to live in a new way."[2] This gradual process of transformation is powered by God himself. We must live accordingly.

Paul is reminding the Colossians that the divisions that mattered when they were living their old lives before Christ are no longer their most important identifying factors. Barbarians were non-Greeks who were generally considered uncultured people. Their name, "barbarian," is a word that echoes what their speech sounded like to Greeks—"bar bar bar." Scythians came from the area of the Black Sea and were considered to be savages. These were substantive differences during this time period that would have certainly prevented relationship between these groups. Paul tells the Colossian church that their membership in the new humanity formed by Christ is their primary identity, therefore allowing them to be united.

Verses 12-14. Paul now uses the image of putting on clothing that reflects the true identity of "God's chosen ones." It is as if he is saying, "You belong to a new group, so dress like it." Basically, he is instructing them to put on Christ, to put on his attributes and character. He calls for patience and self-control in the face of provocation that probably happened in a community of people with such diverse backgrounds also facing false teaching. The church was to act like who they actually were—chosen by God, set apart, and loved. We hear the echoes in these descriptors of who Israel was—also chosen, holy, and loved by God. They were to bear with or "put up with" each other and forgive just as Jesus forgave

---

[2] Moo, *Letters*, 269.

them. Love was to be the final garment they put on, like a coat that covered all of their other clothing. In that way, their lives would be "hidden with Christ in God" (Colossians 2:4).

We must pause and remember Paul's order, even as he instructs these dear Christians with multiple commands. He does not tell them to do these things in order to be holy or loved, in order to be made new, or even in order to prove their discipleship. Paul is making a radical claim about the Colossian believers and about believers of today. We are literally a new race, a new humanity, a group of people whose spiritual life is currently hidden but will be revealed as exalted with Christ for everyone to see at the last day. And God continues to change us by his power as we stay connected to the preeminent Christ. Therefore, we must act like who we are. We must live out of our secure identity. We "dress" like Christ, the first of our race, who has guaranteed our future. As we exhort one another like the Colossians did, we must tell each other as Paul told them, Act like the new person you are, raised with Christ, a citizen of the kingdom of light, made new and continually being transformed, holy and dearly loved.

Verses 15-17. Everytime the word "you" or "your" appears in these three verses, it is in the plural form. Paul continues to speak here to the Colossian church as a whole about their relationships, explaining to them the implications of their new humanity as they live life together. The peace they've been given with God through Christ's work must be what governs their relationships. The Greek word "rule" includes the idea of settling a dispute, as if it is the peace of Christ that must serve as the referee in their relationships. Christians are never called to live out their faith alone but to learn Jesus and his love within his body, the church.

The church was to constantly be hearing, speaking, and singing God's Word. This did not mean only the elders; everyone in the body was to participate, therefore reminding one another of the truths of all of Scripture, including Jesus's teachings, and warding off the false teachings of those who were trying to infiltrate the church. Did you get that? It is not only the job of the elders and pastors to teach, exhort, counsel, warn, encourage, and instruct the church. We are all to use God's Word actively and wisely to build up the body, paying attention to and listening to one another. We do this sometimes as we sing in worship together, sometimes as we pray, and sometimes in conversation. But in all of these practices we have thankfulness in our hearts.

Paul sums up this passage with a command to do everything in the name of or in line with the character of Jesus. For the new self, the believer who is part of the new humanity, all things must be governed by the character of Christ as we put him on, layer by layer. Again, Paul tells the Colossians to give thanks—the third time he has mentioned thankfulness in these three verses. If we believe that God is the one who has raised us with Christ, made us one with our brothers and sisters in his body, enabled our obedience, and given us real hope for eternity, thankfulness is the correct response.

If you are a believer in Christ, you are united to him, and a part of the body that is growing and being transformed by God. The part of you that was governed by the world has died, though its temptations still surround you. Do not put on the clothes of the sinful world, but instead put on Christ; let his character dress you with compassion and kindness, being patient with each other. Jesus, the preeminent one, the ruler of all, dwells in his people, the church. He says to you individually and to you, plural, his body, This is who you are. Be who you are.

Reflection Questions

4. Paul's first list of sins in verse 5 are linked together as all being examples of idolatry, which is desiring anything more than God. How do you see this in these words? How have you seen idolatry in your life?

5. Paul's second list of sins in verses 8-9 are things that affect relationships in the church. Which do you see the most in yourself? What do you need to repent of?

6. Paul points out major group differences of that time in history and tells them that they are no longer these things "but Christ is all, and in all." What group divisions do we currently see in the church? How can Paul's words help us think differently about that?

7. Paul calls the peace of Christ to act almost as a referee in relationships. Give an example of a time you have seen the peace of Christ function in this way?

8. Many believers feel like they have been required to live a life of virtue but don't feel like they have been empowered to do so. Have you felt empowered by the Spirit to do the things God has asked of you? Why or why not?

Focus verse: *Put on then, as God's chosen ones, holy and beloved, compassionate hearts, kindness, humility, meekness, and patience, bearing with one another and, if one has a complaint against another, forgiving each other; as the Lord has forgiven you, so you also must forgive. And above all these put on love, which binds everything together in perfect harmony.*
Colossians 3:12-14

Reflections, curiosities, frustrations:

Study 9

A New Humanity

Read Colossians 3:18–4:6

Observation Questions

1. What specific commands did Paul give to various people in Colossians 3:18–4:1?

2. What does Paul ask them to pray for in chapter 4, verses 3-4?

3. In chapter 4, verses 2 and 5-6 he gives more instructions. What are they?

Interpretation

Believe it or not, Paul is *still* working out the implications of these brothers and sisters having been raised with Christ and a part of a new humanity in which Christ is the firstfruits. In the previous section he worked through what that reality meant for their relationships in the church. Next, he will explore what their new life means for everyday relationships in their homes. If we are in Christ, these principles are true for us as well. The supremacy of Jesus means everything in our lives must be ordered around him, including our closest relationships.

Chapter 3, verses 18–21. Before getting into the specifics, we must understand the form Paul is using here. In the Greco-Roman world, most people would have been quite familiar with something called household codes. These were laws that invested power in the fathers of each household and instructed them about how to rule everyone under their roof. Paul uses this form, but transforms it into a Christocentric household code. Notice the use of the word "Lord"–eight times in verses 3:18–4:1 ("master" is translated from the same Greek base: *kurios*). Paul only uses this word six other times in the entire letter. He is impressing upon these brothers and sisters that the lordship of Jesus must influence every relationship.

Study 9: A New Humanity (Col. 3:18–4:6)

In order to rightly understand verse 18, we must first divest it of all of the misunderstanding and baggage with which it has been burdened. This verse has been used to abuse women for centuries as men have used words, fists, and even legal power to oppress their wives and unleash their cruelty. None of that was Paul's intention. In fact, while the Greco-Roman household codes would have addressed only men and empowered them to do whatever necessary to get their households under control, Paul dignifies women by addressing them at all in verse 18. Paul is appealing to these women to put themselves voluntarily under the leadership of their husbands, only because Jesus is their ultimate authority. Verse 18 is not a command for all women to submit to all men everywhere but is directed to the marriage relationship.

No other ancient code required men to love their wives. Again, Paul takes this cultural form and uses it to paint a picture of the household Jesus desires for his children. Unlike the heads of the Roman state who lorded their power over everyone under them, anyone in authority in the new humanity must follow the example of Christ's leadership. This means the goal of their authority is not power and control but self-sacrifice and the good of those under them. Jesus expressed his authority by dying for his bride, the church. This is the calling for men as the heads of households. They must put the needs of their wives ahead of their own. They must make their wives' well-being and health a priority. They must not oppress or become bitter, exercising authority the way the world does. It is possible that Paul's words require our attention in the places men and women struggle: women in respecting their husbands, and men in putting the needs of their wives before their own.

Again Paul goes against his culture's norms by addressing children at all, treating them as if they have agency and a choice about their behavior. Fathers are to make it as easy as possible for their children to obey by their treatment of them. Fathers are not to

81

irritate or exasperate their children by belittling or neglecting them so that they grow resentful to the point of being discouraged or losing heart.

Chapter 3, verses 22–25, and chapter 4, verse 1. Here again we must divest Paul's words of their meaning in our context. The slavery of which Paul speaks was not the terrible, dehumanizing practice of chattel slavery that occurred when Africans were kidnapped, made to work for nothing, and abused in the United States. "Bondservant" was a much wider category in this era, including some born into slavery, some captured in war, and some who sold themselves into slavery to repay a debt. This slavery was not based on race or skin color, and slaves were often treated well in the places of their service. Many were doctors, teachers, and businesspeople. Some historians estimate that up to one-third of the entire population of Rome was a slave in this way.

Paul commands this group of bondslaves who would have certainly been represented in the church to obey the masters they have on earth, not only when they are looking, but when no one is looking. They are to obey from the heart, ultimately fearing their heavenly master, Jesus. Ultimately, says Paul, when you work, you are working for the Lord. You will receive your inheritance from Jesus himself. Most slaves would not expect any type of earthly inheritance. But in an echo of the Old Testament promise to his people to give them land, Paul speaks of these believing slaves' inheritance in Christ—the kingdom of God and salvation. Because of the preeminence of Christ, he is our ultimate Lord and master. He is the one we finally serve, no matter what man or woman we answer to here on earth.

The status of slavery would not exempt these men and women from the requirement to do right and to work well for their masters. "There is no partiality," meaning God doesn't play favorites. On the flip side, masters must treat their slaves with justice because they, too, were slaves. Those in the church were slaves to Christ and had the same Lord. Though Paul never endorses slavery, he reshapes the relationships of those within it. Paul puts slaves and masters on equal footing spiritually with their identity in Christ, regardless of their social status. He commands them to put on Christ and imitate him even in this part of their lives.

While we no longer work as slaves or employ slaves, we may apply this passage to our relationships in the workplace. This is often where the rubber meets the road for believers. Those in places of authority will answer to Jesus about how they treated their workers, how they paid them, and how they spoke to them. The pastor who gave wonderful sermons but bullied or verbally abused his staff will answer to Jesus for his actions. The attorney who smooth-talked her way through court cases but was cruel to her legal assistant will give an account to Jesus.

But also, those under authority will also have to answer for their actions. The middle manager who held back some of their earnings from their boss will be held accountable. For all who belong to him, Jesus is the true master. It is very possible that Paul writes so much about slaves because of the presence of Onesimus, a slave and member of the Colossian church being sent back to his master, also a member of the church, by Paul (see the book of Philemon in its entirety).

Chapter 4, verses 2-6. Paul has worked his way through church relationships and home relationships. Now, what about relationships with the outside world? How should the fullness of Christ affect those? First, it should result in consistent prayer. This does not mean constant prayer all day long but a persistent and steady habit of prayer. Specifically, he commends thanksgiving in their prayers, and a watchfulness, probably against false teaching like that invading the Colossian church.

The "mystery of Christ" Paul mentions is the same as the mystery he spoke of earlier in the letter (1:27, 2:2). This is what was hidden for ages, meaning not fully revealed but now clear in the life, death, resurrection, and indwelling of Christ in the church. Paul wants these brothers and sisters to pray that even though he is in prison, a door would open for God's Word to get to more people. Notice that Paul doesn't ask them to pray he would be released. For Paul, the circumstance of prison does not impede, and in fact could even advance, as it did in Philippians, the spread of the gospel message. Paul knew he had been ordained by God to be a part of the revelation of the mystery of Christ as he preached this message to the Gentiles. He wanted the Word to be proclaimed clearly.

The supremacy and lordship of Christ also had implications for the Colossians' actions and speech around unbelievers. First, they must use wisdom, living in a way that would contribute to the sharing of the gospel. Generosity and kindness toward your next door neighbor paves the way for relationship and gospel sharing in a way that relational retreat and rigidity about property lines never could. Their speech with outsiders was to be salty, tasteful, and preserving of the good. They should be ready with answers for their unbelieving friends and associates.

All of this assumes outsiders would have questions in the first place. Paul assumes that the lives of these believers would stand out and be different than those around them. He expects that as they put to death sexual immorality, impurity, and covetousness and put away anger, malice, slander, and obscene talk, the people around them will notice. He anticipates that when they treat Jews, barbarians, and slaves as equals in a culture that holds them separate and at different levels of worth, neighbors will take note. Paul hopes that when these brothers and sisters know how they've been loved and chosen and therefore put on humility, kindness, patience, and love, forgiving one another, outsiders will see something different in them. They'll meet wives who speak respectfully about their husbands even when they're not around. They'll see men loving their wives and putting their needs first instead of abusing their authority. They'll see slaves working for their earthly masters with sincerity of heart. And all of these things will cause others to ask, Why are you different? Where does your gratitude come from? These are the questions the Colossians, and we today, should be ready to answer.

Many have used the popular quote from Abraham Kuyper, "There is not a square inch in the whole domain of our human existence over which Christ, who is Sovereign over all, does not cry: 'Mine!'" Paul has applied Christ's sovereignty to the Colossians' church, home, and relationships with unbelievers. If he were to enter our homes or workplaces, he might ask us, Have you centered all of your relationships and priorities around money? Status? Fear? Pleasing other people? Reputation or what they might think? Then he would boldly remind you, Live as who you are. You are a holy, beloved child of God who has risen with Christ, who is above all things. Be who you are!

Reflection Questions

4. Paul calls the Colossian believers to demonstrate the lordship of Christ through their self-sacrifice to others they are in relationship with. What specific differences have you seen when this is done by wives, husbands, fathers, and children?

5. Re-read the commentary on chapter 3, verses 18-21 again. Often instructions toward women in the Scripture, like submission, have been misused or misunderstood. How does learning the cultural context about these verses give you new insight?

6. Often people have used the mention of slavery in biblical texts to support the slavery that was used in America. Why is learning the true biblical context so important? How does this change your understanding of these verses?

7. Paul asks them to pray for God to open a door for them to share the Word but does not ask them to pray for him to be released from prison. This demonstrates a focus on a higher calling and a contentment to walk that out, which is all enabled by the Holy Spirit. Where currently in your life do you need the Lord's help to get you to that level of contentment?

8. Paul calls them to lean on Jesus's supremacy in their life to "work heartily, as for the Lord and not for men, knowing that from the Lord you receive the inheritance as your reward." Do you struggle with this instruction? Why?

9. Paul encourages them to interact in relationships with outsiders a certain way. When have you seen believers do this and make an impact on unbelievers? When have you seen them not heed these words and it has been hurtful and unhelpful?

Focus verse: *Whatever you do, work heartily, as for the Lord and not for men, knowing that from the Lord you will receive the inheritance as your reward. You are serving the Lord Christ.*
Colossians 3:23–24

Reflections, curiosities, frustrations:

Study 10

Paul's Friends and Fellow Workers

Read Colossians 4:7–18

Observation Questions

1. How many people does Paul reference in verses 7-18? And to whom else does he ask that they read this letter?

2. In verses 12-13, Paul talks about their pastor, Epaphras. What does he say about him?

3. In verse 17 what is the specific statement Paul wants to be relayed to Archippus?

Interpretation

Paul has finished his teaching and training at this point in his letter. But we must remember that he was writing to real people with real relationships. In this last portion, we learn a little about Paul's circumstances and life in the early church. The fellowship of these brothers and sisters challenges and encourages us in our own attempts to live a life worthy of Christ.

Verses 7-9. Unlike our modern experience, there was no mail service in Paul's day. In order to deliver his letter, Paul enlisted Tychicus who may have been originally from Ephesus. This was not Tychicus's first work with Paul. He carried Paul's letter to Titus (Titus 3:12) and accompanied Paul to Jerusalem (Acts 20:4). It is probable that Paul also sent his letters to the Ephesians and to Philemon with Tychicus on the same trip. Because of his relationship with Paul and his work as a "faithful minister and fellow servant in the Lord," Tychicus would not only have carried letters but also would have filled in informational gaps for the recipients. Paul writes in verse 8, "that you may know how we are." Tychicus would have answered many questions for the Colossians about Paul, whom they had never met. He also would have encouraged their hearts, probably helping to apply the truths written in Paul's letter in specific and personal ways.

Onesimus was a slave of one of the Colossian Christians, Philemon. Though we're not given his full story, we know Onesimus came to faith through Paul during Paul's imprisonment. Though he was still a slave economically to Philemon, Onesimus was now a "beloved brother" of Paul, and a fellow servant of Christ.

Verses 10-13. As Paul goes on, we learn more about the network of relationships that had grown among these brothers in the midst of their faith and ministry. Aristarchus was apparently in prison with Paul. His name was mentioned in Acts 19:29 as one who was with Paul in the riot at Ephesus. We know a little bit more about Mark, Barnabas's cousin. Years before, Barnabas and Paul had delivered some money given by the church in Antioch to the saints in Jerusalem, where they met Mark. Mark then went with them on their first missionary journey but abandoned the work in Pamphylia. Because of this, Paul didn't want to take Mark on his second missionary journey. Barnabas disagreed, leading to a split between Barnabas and Paul. At some point these two men must have reconciled since we get Paul's words to the Colossians instructing them to welcome Mark. Peter also mentions Mark in 1 Peter 5:13 and names him as his "son," obviously a beloved partner in ministry.

It was common in the first-century multilingual world for Jews to take a second name of Greek or Roman origin. Therefore, Jesus (a common Jewish name at the time) goes by Justus. Paul names Aristarchus, Mark, and Justus as his three present Jewish coworkers. They have "been a comfort" to Paul. It is easy to imagine Paul as a strong, fearless disciple in all of his travels and preaching. But Paul lived through extremely difficult circumstances and undoubtedly became tired, discouraged, and anxious just like any other disciple of Christ. He needed encouragement, compassion, and the comfort of friends. These men had been those things for him as they worked together preaching the gospel and training disciples.

Epaphras was from Colossae and prayed for the Colossians energetically and consistently. The Greek word translated "struggling" has athletic connotations that help us understand this man wrestled with God in his pleas for the Colossian church. He contended for the gospel and its work among them. He longed for them to be mature and steadfast in their faith. Paul uses strong language here to impress upon the brothers and sisters in Colossae that Epaphras has "worked hard" for them and for those in Laodicea and Hierapolis. All three churches were probably founded by Epaphras, a keen pastor who interceded strenuously and persistently for these churches. What a comfort to these saints to know their undershepherd was constantly praying for them.

Verses 14–16. Luke was a dear friend and companion of Paul. He spent many years ministering alongside him, as we learn from Philemon 24 and 2 Timothy 4:11, and was probably with Paul when he died. Demas was with Paul at this time but sadly did not stay. We read in 2 Timothy 4:10, "For Demas, in love with this present world, has deserted me and gone to Thessalonica." Again we realize with these personal histories that these were real people, fragile and fallen. They argued, made plans, got tired, needed encouragement, and relied on each other.

Laodicea, as mentioned before, was only about nine miles from Colossae and probably had another church begun by Epaphras. Since there were no church buildings, Christians had to open their houses as worship centers where the saints could gather to sing and listen to the Scriptures. Nympha was probably a wealthy widow who hosted the church at Laodicea. Paul repeats the word "read" three times in verse 16, commanding that his letters to the churches at Laodicea and Colossae be switched and read to each congregation. Paul must have believed that his letters were relevant and helpful in their theological teaching not only for the intended recipients but also for other Christians.

Verses 17-18. Though we don't get details, we can assume from the context that Archippus had some sort of ministry related to the Laodicean or Colossian church. This man is named in Philemon 2 as a "fellow soldier." He had been given an assignment or duty of some kind from the Lord, and Paul wanted to encourage him to fulfill or "make complete" what had already begun. This is not a form letter to an unknown group of people. Each person named needs something different: some to be welcomed, some encouraged, some recognized as trustworthy. Paul patiently dictates each name and situation as he finishes his letter. To Paul, the individual people he is addressing are as important as the truths about which he is writing.

It was common practice in the ancient world to hire a trained scribe for letter writing purposes. These people could write small letters neatly, which saved expensive papyrus while making the words easier to read. In order to authenticate his letters and prove that he was indeed the author, Paul signed with his own hand. He finished by mentioning his chains, using a word for "remember" that also meant "call to mind," probably suggesting they mention his chains in their prayers. He ends his letter with grace.

Paul began his letter to these dear sisters and brothers by explaining the preeminence or supremacy of Christ. He walked them through the new life they had been given because of their union with Jesus. He then applied those two truths to every aspect of their lives: false teaching, forgiveness, ascetic practices, sin habits, new holy habits, relationships in the church and at home, and attitudes toward outsiders. These truths are just as life-altering for us as they were in the first century. The supremacy of Christ and our union with him today changes everything.

Christ is enough to make us new, change our habits, and help us perceive false and true teaching. Christ is sufficient to enable our putting off of old sin habits and putting on of his character. The fullness of Christ as he dwells in the church is enough that we might love each other there. He is sufficient for husbands to love their wives and wives to submit to their husbands, and for us all to love the outsider and walk wisely among them. In all things, Christ is preeminent. In all things, he is sufficient. Beloved, lean into what he has already given you.

Reflection Questions

4. Paul mentions Tychicus, who is more than just a mailman for Paul but also answers the church's questions when he hand delivers their letters to them. This seemingly small job was crucial and deserved Paul's acknowledgement. How does this show the importance of all types of service to the church?

5. The way Paul references Mark shows that reconciliation has happened with him after the conflict we were made aware of in Acts. What hope does this give you about conflict with other believers? What situation in your life currently needs this encouragement?

6. Even the great apostle Paul needed the comfort from his friends to walk out his life's calling. How has this been critical in your life as well? If this has not been your experience, what practically can you do to seek this type of friendship out?

7. The Colossian church's pastor, Epaphras, wrestled with God in prayer for his people and longed for their maturity. Have you ever had a pastor like this? What impact did that relationship have on you?

8. While we don't know why Paul sent a direct message encouraging Archippus, it could have been because he was feeling incapable or ill-equipped. When has someone spoken direct, specific, encouraging words to you that gave you the confidence to walk out something God asked you to do?

9. What are your main take-aways from studying the book of Colossians?

Focus verse: *I have sent him to you for this very purpose, that you may know how we are and that he may encourage your hearts.*
Colossians 4:8

Reflections, curiosities, frustrations:

Works Cited

Bauer, Walter. *A Greek-English Lexicon of the New Testament and Other Early Christian Literature.* 3rd edition, revised and edited by Frederick William Danker. Chicago: University of Chicago Press, 2001.

Beale, G.K. *Colossians and Philemon.* Baker Exegetical Commentary on the New Testament. Grand Rapids, MI: Baker Academic, 2019.

Ferguson, Sinclair. "Solid Joys and Treasures." Sermon. First Presbyterian Church, Columbia, SC. August 6, 2006.

Moo, Douglas J. *The Letters to the Colossians and to Philemon.* The Pillar New Testament Commentary, general editor D.A. Carson. Grand Rapids, MI: William B. Eerdmans Publishing Company, 2008.

Thompson, Alan J. *Colossians and Philemon.* Tyndale New Testament Commentaries, volume 12. Downers Grove, IL: IVP Academic, 2022.

Wright. N.T. *Colossians and Philemon.* Tyndale New Testament Commentaries, volume 12. Downers Grove, IL: IVP Academic, 1986.

Acknowledgments

Hope: Ray-Ray, thanks for your constant love, laughter, and support! Thank you, ladies of Trinity Grace Church of San Antonio, for walking through the pilot of this book with me. You guys were a delight, and you helped me know what to tweak and change. Chris, thanks for always being up for whatever I want to do—I love doing this with you. Nae, you will always and forever will be the wonderwoman of editing. Jen, man so many things, but thank you most for the prayers all the time about all the things, including every detail of this study. To my three dogs, thanks for all the support by way of cuddles. Jesus, this book highlights our union with you, which I still don't fully grasp and yet am so thankful for. I love you.

Chris: Michael, thank you again for your patience with my many questions and for being my favorite person. To the little group of women at Sarah McDaniel's house, thank you for walking through a pilot study with me with such grace and openness. Dr. Brad Matthews, thank you for being so generous with your time and knowledge, especially while holding down two other jobs. Hope, Renae, and Jen, you're the best part of doing this. I still can't believe we get to do it.

Other At His Feet Studies

We pray that you will continue to sit at the feet of Jesus, studying his Word. To help you with this, we have also written Bible studies on these books of the Bible:

Romans (28 studies)

1 Samuel (16 studies)

Philippians (12 studies)

Psalms (13 studies)

Luke: Part 1 (13 studies)

Luke: Part 2 (14 studies)

Luke: Part 3 (12 studies)

The Servant King: A Study of the Gospel of Luke (10 studies)

Galatians (8 studies)

Gálatas (8 studies)

Lamentations (7 studies)

Made in the USA
Coppell, TX
24 August 2024

36385145R00069